The Rats

of Nationalism

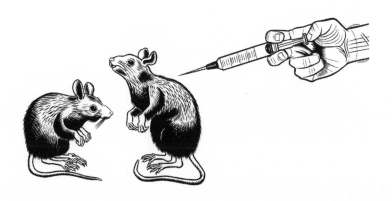

Brandon Adamson

Cover Illustrations by Mark Velard

Briny Books

Phoenix, AZ USA

ISBN-13: 978-0-578-58474-4

Dedicated to all the wounded animals who've been released back into the wild, so that they may one day find their way home.

CONTENTS

The Rats of Nationalism

INTRODUCTION

"We can no longer live as rats. We know too much." - *Nicodemus,*
The Secret of NIMH

For a brief time when I was a child, I went through a
bizarre phase where I became obsessed with the animated Don
Bluth film, *The Secret of NIMH*, which had aired repeatedly on
HBO in 1983 and 1984. I also had it recorded on a Beta
videocassette tape (yes, that's how long ago this was). The movie
was an adaptation of the 1971 book, *Mrs. Frisby and the Rats of*
NIMH (which itself was loosely inspired by the well known
"mousetopia" and rat experiments of researcher John C Calhoun).
Anyway, to those not familiar, the story of *The Secret of NIMH*
concerns a group of escaped laboratory rats who became intelligent
as a result of experiments conducted upon them at a facility known
as NIMH (National Institute of Mental Health). The rats were able
to read and talk, and, soon after escaping in the middle of the night,
they built their own "advanced" civilization (complete with
elevators and electricity) within a rosebush on a small country farm.

I was so fascinated by this concept as a kid that I took a
bunch of my toys out to the bushes in our front yard and attempted
to construct a "habitat" for the rats to come and live in. Nevermind

the fact that there were no rats anywhere in our yard, only the occasional chipmunk or squirrel. I left the toy structures in the bushes for who knows how many weeks or months, but no rats (intelligent or otherwise) ever moved in.

What I would never have guessed at that time, however, is that 35 years later, I and other politically active individuals would find ourselves in a similar situation to that of the rats of NIMH, as unknowing subjects of an elaborate infiltration, pacification and deradicalization program, conducted most likely by elements within our own government. For who knows how long, those of us involved in alternative political movements may have been subjects of psychological experiments, prodding, probing and social manipulation, the details and full extent of which we may never know.

Before reading on, I feel obligated to tell you that this is not one of those heavily researched "bombshell" books filled with classified documents and secret formulas. Indeed, I have no documented, verifiable evidence of any kind for many of the claims I'm going to make. It's all what I would call "informed" speculation, if you get my drift. Anyone familiar with my writing knows I have never been a conspiracy guy. I never was a fan of Alex Jones and have never found the arguments supporting common conspiracy theories to be particularly convincing, whether we're talking about the JFK assassination, 9/11 Trutherism, the Illuminati, Sandy Hook, flat earth, the moon landing, Roswell, "pizzagate" or any of that crap.

Since I'm not generally one of those types and in order to maintain *some* credibility with other "skeptics," I will not go any further than simply say what I *think* is happening. That's it. Nothing more, nothing less. What I believe I *can* do, though, is convey my thoughts in ways which intelligent, *authentic* individuals in alternative political movements will understand. If you happen to be one of these people, you're the target audience of this book. Many of the things I say will make sense to you, and you will *believe them.*

Let me also state up front that I don't identify with any particular faction of the dissident right. I'm on fairly good terms with people from every one of the rival cliques (wignats, amnats, ironybros, frogtwitter, anti-woke left, etc.), but I've never really chosen a "side" or felt that I fit in anywhere. I've become less interested in ideological differences over the last couple of years, and these days, I'm *much more* invested in determining whether or not someone is real than in highlighting the specific areas of our political disagreement. There are genuine individuals and subversive infiltrators in every sector of nearly every political movement.

Above all, though, you should probably not take this speculative odyssey *too* seriously. It should be viewed more as an abstract, meditative endeavor than anything else. Not everyone shares an appreciation for abstract art, even when it may have a fair street value.

GALLERY OF INFORMERS

Several years ago I had an art show at a small gallery in downtown Phoenix called Conspire. I'm not even sure to what extent you could have called the venue a "gallery." It was more of a small cafe, which had an art component to it. The show itself was nothing special. It was a group show, and those of us who participated had a few paintings on display in various rooms. The gallery, Conspire, closed down at some point not too long after that and was replaced by some similarly bohemian joint, as is often the case with these kinds of arts district establishments. They come and go.

At this point, you're probably wondering where I'm going with this anecdote, and what it could possibly have to do with the price of tea in Washington DC, so I'll just get right down to the nitty gritty. Conspire had an anarchist presence to it, and some of its employee staff members and their associates were active locally in the "Occupy Wall Street" protest movement, which was fashionably rebellious at the time. That would not seem very remarkable on the surface, except that it was later revealed that local protest participants and organizers were being extensively monitored and tracked by both the feds and local law enforcement.

As Monica Alonzo reported for the Phoenix New Times in 2011:

> The Phoenix cop attended public group meetings but
> also spent time with organizers in the park and on
> other occasions to gather details about protests and
> report them to superiors.
>
> At the same time, an analyst with the PPD's
> Homeland Defense Bureau, part of the fusion center,
> monitored Occupy protesters' Facebook and Twitter
> accounts or used advanced technologies, such as
> facial recognition, to identify members of the
> movement.
>
> (Alonzo)

There was even infiltration attempted within the gallery itself:

> A clean-cut man with slicked-back salt-and-pepper
> hair who appeared to be in his 50s introduced
> himself to activists in early 2011 while they were
> gathered at Conspire, a now-closed coffee shop and
> vegan cafe, Hodai's report states.

Although certain activists believed all along that he was a cop, the man claimed to be a homeless Mexican with ties to anarchists in that country. Public records show that after getting chummy with those attending Occupy gatherings, the man, who indeed turned out to be a cop, would report back any information about the group's future plans to his supervisors.

(Alonzo)

When a friend initially alerted me to these revelations, it was all very eye-opening for me because the story hit so close to home.

While I was never involved in local activism of any kind, those being tracked were only one degree away from my own social circles. I had naively assumed that being monitored by the feds was something reserved for lunatic members of "weekend warrior" militia groups and swarthy foreigners suspected of having ties to Islamic terrorist organizations, not hippy baristas, open-mic slam poets and vegan sandwich artists.

The implications of these revelations are even more disturbing to me now, though. If coordinated local/federal counter-terrorism task forces were willing expend such substantial resources and manpower toward disrupting these milquetoast "Occupy" protests and infiltrating a teeny tiny Phoenix art gallery, then just imagine how much energy they must be devoting toward thwarting more genuinely radical and "revolutionary" movements such as the AltRight, neoreaction and even antifa. To add insult to injury, Americans' own tax dollars are largely funding these busybody monitors and their manipulative operations. I don't want to focus on the money, though. I'm not a libertarian anyway. I'm more interested in exploring/exposing the nature of the current infiltrations we face, and by "we" I mean anyone perceived to be involved in the dissemination of controversial political ideas of any kind.

ENTANGLED IN CANDY LAND

Like almost every wide eyed 80s kid, I have vague childhood memories of playing the classic board game, *Candy Land*, which enjoyed a resurgence in popularity at that time after the iconic 1984 version was released. Usually I played the game with my cousin at her house on quiet days during summer vacation. I don't remember much about it except that I was fond of the aesthetics of the board and the cards.

However, my nostalgia for the game was recently reactivated when my friend Pilleater (Francis Nally) made a brief video about the nature of the game. He pointed out how there is "no strategy involved," and that the outcome of the *Candy Land* is predetermined by "the shuffle of the cards." The game creates the *illusion* that players are making conscious choices to advance their position (*"'Winning' and Candy Land."*) Really though, all they are doing is mindlessly drawing cards and taking their cues from the top of the deck. Players are distracted from the fact they are not actually affecting anything, by the board's captivating artwork and enchanting locations as they eagerly anticipate each tantalizing new card.

The more I thought about it, the more I began to see the game of *Candy Land* as a metaphor for any situation where someone perceives that their actions and decisions are meaningfully influencing the course of events, but in actuality those actions are being directed and manipulated within a controlled environment by outside forces. In such scenarios, the participants are merely going through the motions on a predestined path, like "drivers" of matchbox cars being pushed along on a toy race track toward a generic finish line, one with no checkered flag, no trophy girl and no **Big Red chewing gum** commercial make-out session waiting for them. Really, no reward of any kind except a brief hit of dopamine.

A good example would be like being an executive for a penny stock company that is being pumped and dumped by powerful outside investor groups. No matter what management decisions you make or how well you perform your job, it will have almost no effect on the stock price since it is being heavily manipulated by these shadowy investors through bogus press releases, mass email campaigns and other manufactured hype schemes. It may be a fun ride watching the stock soar and dive, but at the end of the day all you really are is a pinksheet, paper shuffling, gingerbread man in *Candy Land*.

Recently I've come to a startling realization that being active in nationalist or "AltRight" political movements is also analogous to being entangled in a game of *Candy Land*. Participants who think they're consciously forming and advancing their own narrative are in fact constantly being nudged ideologically in various directions by actors and saboteurs with social media clout. Labels like "thought leader" and "influencer" are unintentionally revealing in terms of what they can potentially signify.

Just as the marketing tagline for *Candy Land* is "a child's first game," there's a certain child-like innocence to political sincerity, to being enamored and excited by the prospect of encountering ideologically like-minded individuals, to genuine interaction and earnest conviction, to a persistent willingness to follow a far-fetched premise through to its fruition, and in picturing the world as a dreamlike wonderland, ripe with budding possibilities around each new corner. There's a sweet, reverse **Sour Patch Kid** sense of awe and wonder that often fades to a bitter **black licorice** pill with the age and experience that comes from participating in dissident politics for a lengthy period of one's life.

Like lemmings, many people in these online dissident communities get caught up chasing wave after wave of manufactured memes. Collectively distracted from the determined pursuit of authentic political goals, they find themselves getting bogged down in the Gooey **Gumdrops** of vapid entertainment, performative irony, and mindless shitposting. Instead of being lost in the **Lollipop** Woods (until a BLUE card is drawn), mesmerized by the surrounding scenery and enamored with the pristine nubility of Princess Lolly, or perhaps being taken in by the icy cool and calculated charms of a blonde-haired, blue-eyed, Queen Frostine... in this case they're caught up in the "a e s t h e t i c s" of an *extremely online* world, and reduced to regurgitating the latest viral meme mantras and cornball lingo that's been pre-packaged, shrinkwrapped and spoon-fed to them, straight from the imageboard "meme factory" cesspools, Discord honeypots and compromised group chats. People just gobble it up like candy... Miles of **rope licorice** to tie themselves to the bedpost with. Just go through the motions, and you'll be rewarded with clout. To paraphrase an old saying, *never look a **Pez** dispenser in the mouth.*

There is a familiar trope which often was jokingly repeated around these circles a few years ago. It goes, "Maybe the real treasure was the friends we made along the way," with some variations replacing the word "treasure" with "ethnostate" or whatever else is relevant to the topic being discussed, the implication being that the experiences on the journey are potentially more valuable than the reward which awaits upon reaching your goal. That might as well be a metaphor for this phenomenon.

What you have to remember though is that the goal *is* the most important thing, and some of those "friends" you meet along the way aren't *really* your friends...

They're there specifically to lead you astray, away from your dreams and to make sure that you remain entangled in a glow in the dark game of *Candy Land*.

THE RATS OF NATIONALISM

"No, I'm all right. Or am I?

Why don't I just simply and clinically find out?"

[Yells out to the crowd] "Oh, I'm shot!"

[Falls down as if dead]

"I was right. I'm not paranoid. They're all spies!"

- James Coburn as Dr. Sidney Schaefer in The President's Analyst

We all know the type. His profile decked out in swastikas and other Third Reich iconography, the aggressive, surly extremist on social media who constantly advocates for violence (i.e. "fedposting"). The guy who LARPs as a Hollywood Nazi at public demonstrations and makes outrageously offensive statements in order to make nationalism appear kooky and repulsive to ordinary people. The archetypal agent provocateur, who often baits political dissidents into plotting illegal, terrorist activities so that he can subsequently entrap these misguided individuals. All of the preceding cases represent various examples of the familiar conception of the "federal infiltrator," and have come to be accepted as common knowledge in alternative political movements. Depending on a movement's ideological leanings and political goals, the tangible forms may differ, but the blueprint for the actor is still more or less the same. This characterization of a "fed" is widely recognized and commentators like Ramzpaul frequently warn people to avoid associating with those who exhibit these types of behaviors. This breed of federal infiltration agents most certainly exists, and there have been plenty of documented cases of people being arrested and charged with serious crimes resulting from incriminating statements they've made to federal agents whom they were unknowingly interacting with. Even if this particular sort of trope is partially or totally exaggerated, avoiding people who seem criminally insane and/or sociopathic is almost always good advice, *whether they're feds or not.*

What if I told you, though, that there's *another* type of fed you might not be aware of? A type you would not suspect because their goals and modus operandi do not correlate with what you've come to associate with known "fed" behavior. If you're active (even in a limited capacity) in political circles of any kind on social media, there's a very good chance you're following and interacting with this type of fed regularly, without even realizing it. Rather than attempt to entice someone into committing an illegal act or disrupt a movement's image by using extreme, off-putting rhetoric, this type of fed inserts himself into the equation at *earlier* stages in the radicalization process for the purpose of pacification. They infiltrate these movements not to "bust" people, but to get in positions where they can monitor and influence the direction in ways which maintain *balance*. They want to prevent things from getting out of hand, so they aim to redirect potentially revolutionary energies back toward a more benign ideological territory, one which poses less of a threat to the framework of the existing political order.

Once you realize this, then you begin to understand. Instead of taking the familiar form of violent, LARPing lunatics, such feds will often present as sensible, clean-cut and reasonable figures. Unsurprisingly, these types can more easily gain substantial followings on social media and become elevated into influential positions of organizational leadership, etc... where they can exercise a greater degree of control over messaging and the framing of ideas. They can then utilize their clout to affect and moderate the views of those within their circles, preventing individuals from drifting *too far* into extremism. Again, the intent isn't to bust people, but rather to reach them ideologically at a point early enough where they can still be nudged in a more docile direction. Think of it as a *proactive* rather than *reactive* management style. This preemptive maneuvering is preferable to a last resort, reactive scenario, where the feds have to attempt to contain an individual who's reached the "point of no return," violent lunatic threshold of radicalization whereby they represent an imminent danger. On the surface, this wouldn't even seem all that bad from a nationalist perspective. In addition to the prevention of senseless acts of terrorism, keeping potential nutjobs from going off the deep end would theoretically provide a beneficial sanitation service for these movements, rather than act as *hindrance* to their ascendancy. The more disturbing aspect though is the realization that the people you're interacting with aren't *real* and aren't genuinely working toward the same political goals as you. Turns out these aren't the "friends you made along the way," but treacherous saboteurs looking to construct an invisible "glass ceiling" for your ideological movement, ensuring it never rises to a level where its aspirations could be implemented.

It's important to note here that *some* of these clean cut and presentable infiltrators make a pointed effort to turn people *against* those well spoken, fashionable and charismatic figures who *are* authentic. They always throw out just enough red meat statements to remain sufficiently edgy (not very difficult in today's hyper-PC climate) and retain credibility in the dissident community, while slowly moderating as they gain more followers. They will take advantage of any bad press, minor setback or gaffe to reduce the influence of genuine thought leaders, anything to take them down a notch. As a diversion and means to sow doubt and mistrust, they even go so far as to insist that the authentic people *themselves* are feds. With such large followings of gullible lemmings and a substantial network of their own conscious actors, it is fairly easy for these agents to meme anything into the public consciousness (as we can see from the abundance of absolute nonsense that gets virally absorbed into the social lexicon).

The 1975 science fiction film, *Rollerball* (the original, not the awful 2002 remake) concerns itself with a future in which the world is ruled by giant corporations. The general public, having been largely reduced to a class of pacified consumers, is enamored with a wildly popular global sport called "rollerball," which is essentially a more violent and gladiatorial incarnation of the game we know as *roller derby*. One of the game's star players, "Jonathan E" (played by James Caan) becomes curious as to why he's being aggressively pressured to retire. What the public doesn't know— and what Jonathan slowly comes to find out—is that the game of rollerball exists merely to serve a "social purpose." As executive Bartholomew (John Houseman) explains, "It's not a game that man is supposed to grow strong in." Later he reveals that the game itself "was created to demonstrate the futility of individual effort." Because of Jonathan's charisma and success in the game, the cult of personality around him begins to grow too substantial, to the point where executives perceive his popularity as a threat to their monopoly on social control over the public.

They set Jonathan up with a romantic female partner named Daphne, whom he correctly suspects has been sent to spy on him and "encourage" his behavior in various matters. When he confronts her and suggests she "go get herself another assignment," she simply brushes it off. Rationalizing her actions, she insists, *"Everybody's an assignment. Life's an assignment."* Despite pressures, incentives and threats, Jonathan stubbornly refuses to retire. Therefore, it's determined by the executives that Jonathan E must lose. He must be knocked down a peg in the public's eyes so that his influence and potential to serve as an inspiration for the masses will be diminished.

However dated the film's retrofuturist aesthetics may seem, the paradigm of the story is as relevant as ever and *eerily similar* to the one which dissident individuals find themselves in today. The feds, the government, the powers that be, promote various factions and sub-factions of political dissidents as if they were marketing sports teams in a diversionary game. That's essentially what they're doing, covertly. However, when one of these political figures starts to attract *a little too much* of a following, the feds direct their energy toward reining that person in. They mobilize their resources to play these factions against one another until these groups are reduced to rocking back and forth harmlessly like children on a teeter totter. Social media platforms are modern forms of competitive, "gladiatorial" social spectacles, as is street activism. Ultimately, the feds *want* you to participate and be invested in the game *to a degree,* to have fun, to attain popularity, but only within boundaries which disable your ideas from ever posing a serious challenge to the system itself. Those that veer outside those boundaries will be nudged back in, often unwittingly by former ideological allies who've been "memed" into turning against them.

The feds also want you to entertain yourself into irrelevance. So much of what is pushed on social media is the "fatalistic" notion that there's very little you can do to affect political change. Whether or not this is true is irrelevant to *why* they do it. They don't really want you to try. They're not willing to entertain the risk of what could happen if you do try. "Why are you so concerned with this stuff? There's nothing you can do about it. Things just are the way they are. Your long-term political goals aren't realistic. Just get a good job and go to church and enjoy life." That may or may not be sound advice, but you have to wonder sometimes if the people giving it have your best interests at heart, or whether it's the result of a collective mindfuck, perpetrated by those who get paid to make sure there's no clear winner, and that nobody rocks the boat to the point of it capsizing. Taking *anything seriously at all* has become a socially ostracizing taboo, with entire legions of people ready to mock you for caring about anything besides staying up to date on the latest memes and emojis.

It goes beyond fomenting rivalries. After establishing elbow room for themselves and sufficiently stifling earnest thought leaders, they pivot away from radically ambitious ideas and toward those which fit comfortably within the current order. They pivot to the pursuit of ambitions less disruptive to the existing framework. Witness the coordinated transition from advocating "ethnonationalism" to "American identity," which happened over a very brief period of time. Instead of calling for whites (or any other group) to defiantly and aggressively assert their own collective interests, suddenly we see a massive push for "traditional Catholicism" and to focus on quietly being a productive citizen, cultivating virtue, family values, etc. "Just vote Republican!" Then out of nowhere we see a mass influx of post Alt-Right converts to Catholicism. There is a persuasive case to be made for every single one of these positions, but my intention here is not to debate these issues on their merits. I'm interested in pointing out that the motivations behind their promotion may be insincere.

You might be reading this and thinking to yourself, "What? This is bullshit. I recently became Catholic, and I'm not a federal agent. Reverence for traditional Catholicism is common in reactionary and neoreactionary circles." Let me be clear. I believe that most who convert to Catholicism genuinely embrace the religion. It's not my intention to imply that they don't, and I don't wish to imply that *these ideas themselves* originate with the feds. The thing you have to realize is that the feds are highly intelligent but in a *pencil pusher* kind of way. They are not creative types. They are not artists or dreamers. They are not original thinkers other than in a managerial or strategic sense, as they cleverly concoct schemes to manipulate public opinion and influence behavior. They farm content, copying, boosting and amplifying *existing* material which was created by others.

Whether it's a manifesto, a thoughtful essay, a meme, a clever new term, or even just a profound tweet, the person who originally came up with it most likely was being entirely sincere. The feds just use their network of accounts to prop up ideas, memes and personalities for a time. Once something begins to reach what they deem an excessive level of popularity, they move onto something else, perhaps even a competing idea. They do this to maintain the ideological balance. A friend of mine recently posed the question, "Why is there no Protestant Twitter?" That is *indeed* an interesting question. One possible answer is that the explosive rise of TradCath Twitter was not entirely organic. There's a good chance it was a coordinated op intended to draw people away from the AltRight and steer them toward something perceived as less existentially threatening and less antisocial than outright ethnonationalism. At the very least, it would create a schism (indeed it has!) and fracture the movement into factional irrelevancy.

It would not surprise me if several months from now there suddenly *was* an influx of pro-Protestant memes and Protestant themed social media accounts, just as there has been in the past with paganism, Orthodoxy, etc. as everyone continues to ride the seesaw of pacification. What next? Astrology? Scientology? Who knows? We have already begun to see a collective backlash against LARPy, authoritarian monarchist TradCaths (the kind who actually wish to fundamentally change the way America is governed) by some of the same groups of accounts which only a year ago were paving the way for their rise. I don't want to dwell too much on religion, though, because that's just one of many examples.

We should also examine the proliferation of performative irony and "shitposting" accounts. Many of these seem designed to use ironic humor and witty nonsense to seduce people away from serious ideological pursuits involving potentially "dangerous" concepts or sincere political activism of any kind. This campaign has been largely successful over the past couple of years as quite a few formerly earnest, thoughtful and passionately vocal online activists have transitioned into performative irony/shitposting accounts and have been rewarded with popularity for doing so. Part of this can be attributed to the post-Charlottesville fallout, which resulted in a slew of bad publicity and a massive increase in online censorship. Many people have been forced to "adapt" their online social media presence to be less confrontational and less overtly political. Others were squeamish and weak-willed and some were just turned off by the whole ordeal, stopped caring and moved on. It was nothing but an ideological fad for them that got a little too real, and ugly. Still, we cannot ignore the likely possibility that this trend was cultivated to some degree by those who would stand to benefit from convincing radicalized political dissidents to stop caring about their ideals and instead focus their energy on mindlessly amusing themselves all day. Movement fatigue is real, and apathetic disillusionment among disenchanted activists is a genuine phenomenon. It's also a very conveniently manufactured phenomenon. Both can be true.

Not to get sidetracked here, but a couple of decades ago it was revealed that for a period of at least 20 years, roughly the 1950s-70s, during the Cold War, the CIA secretly funded and promoted the modern art movement worldwide (Saunders, Modern Art Was CIA 'Weapon'). This bombshell revelation is often grossly misrepresented in AltRight circles, partially out of confirmation bias against modern art and partially out of the general ignorance that traditionalists typically evince with regard to 20th century art history. Many conservatives falsely interpret the recently disclosed CIA/modern art connection as proof that modern art was a *creation* of the CIA, that its existence and popularity was *entirely* a deep-state fabrication, unleashed on an unsuspecting public as some kind of cruel psychological joke. "Modern art was just a psyop! You've been had!" The reality is that the CIA merely gave the already well established modern art movement a boost, relatively late in the game at that. Furthermore, they promoted modern art not because they thought it was "bad" or "degenerate," but because doing so bolstered the perception that the US was a bastion of artistic and intellectual freedom, in contrast with the closed-minded totalitarianism of the USSR (Saunders). The Soviets officially favored a more traditional style of painting, which they referred to as "socialist realism." Coincidentally, some of the most famous works of modern art, such as Kazemir Malevich's *Black Square* (1915) and *White On White* (1918), came out of pre-Soviet Russia. It's worth noting that while the Soviet Union didn't care much for abstract expressionist painting, it certainly embraced modern architecture, and all those photographs of the USSR's "drab" communal dwellings and constructivist concrete buildings seem to provide endless fodder for stuffy advocates of "traditionalist" architecture revival. So basically, the narrative is a tad more muddled than it may appear at first glance.

The only reason I bring any of this up is to illustrate that the misrepresentation of this "psyop" has relevance, and not just because I have an appreciation for abstract expressionism and 60s mod fashion. When the feds boost pre-existing ideologies, fads, artists, status updates, whatever, their motivations for doing so are often *counterintuitive* and driven by a broader, overarching initiative, one where the individual fragments may not seem to make much sense without access to the complete picture or *the imagination to visualize it.*

There has also been the recent hype surrounding the book, *Bronze Age Mindset*, by Bronze Age Pervert aka BAP. Despite the book being little more than a mixture of entertainingly bombastic ramblings and rants cobbled together with philosophy (often borrowed from others), it has received a vast amount of coverage from journalists and mainstream media outlets. This improbable surge in publicity all seemed to occur over a relatively brief period. It seems highly unlikely that this monumental spectacle was entirely the result of a groundswell of committed grassroots e-fanatics and "genuine" trolls. The book definitely appears to be getting a signal boost, but from whom, and why? If it is, that doesn't suggest that Bronze Age Pervert is in on it (remember the "pump and dump" penny stock analogy). Based on what is known about BAP's background, it would be highly unlikely. If I had to guess, I would say that he is being promoted as a counterbalancing figure to Richard Spencer, whom he frequently criticizes. Most of the individuals associated with "frogtwitter" (or what remains of it) strike me as legit, but they're clearly being amplified by some outside movers and shakers (where is all the recent funding coming from?) for a reason. Frogtwitter's blend of outlandish intellectualism and clever humor represents a vital force in the reactionary community, and it may be seen *by others* as a useful force within a delicately maintained equilibrium.

Whether we're aware of it or not, so many of us are in the same boat. In an essay for The American Sun (*How The Illuminati Fucked Up My Life*, April 30, 2019), former neoreactionary prodigy Bryce Laliberte wrote at length about his experiences being targeted psychologically by the feds (presumably) and/or other undetermined organizations. Some of Bryce's claims seem far-fetched, and I must admit that as someone who's generally skeptical, when I first read the essay I thought he might have gone completely **Bonkers**. However, that's likely by design. Part of the effect of these psychological tricks is that they induce paranoia. After being subjected to a few coordinated anomalies, you begin to question the legitimacy of *every* interaction and start to read things into *every* unlikely coincidence until—before you know it—you're telling people that the government is messing with your Spotify playlist and has hacked your alarm clock, causing it to go off at inopportune times. They want to get you to a mental state where you find it difficult to function normally or produce meaningful output. They want you to lose credibility by making wild claims and appearing to be out of your gourd.

Bryce Laliberte is no dummy. High-IQ individuals like him will pick up on strange patterns that others miss. The *fundamental* claims he made in his essay strike me as totally believable. They are consistent with some of my own experiences and those of others. When attempting to gauge the validity of these claims, I think it's important to focus on the basic framework and the initial triggering phenomena rather than base your conclusions around bizarre claims which were made *after* the individual has been driven to the edge of madness.

The interesting thing for me is that back when Bryce was a prominent contributor within neoreactionary Catholic circles, I rarely agreed with anything he ever wrote or said. I never realized I had so much in common with him until now. I'm not going to post excerpts or rehash any of Bryce's specific claims, because his essay has since been deleted, and I want to respect his privacy. If you're really curious, it is archived in a couple of places on the web.

Speaking of curiosity, you might be wondering why—in a discussion about infiltration and subversion—I haven't allotted any space to discussing the likes of The Daily Stormer, Andrew Anglin and Weev. The reasons are fairly simple, but I feel as though I might as well mention them. First, I don't really care to get into *Baby-Sitters Club* tier gossip and teenage drama. More importantly —as I alluded to in the beginning of this book—when it comes to certain people, it doesn't *really matter* whether they are feds or Mossad or trolls or completely genuine. When individuals openly and gleefully present themselves as *pond scum*, appealing to the lowest common denominator, and they have a documented history of engaging in lowbrow transgression for its own sake, it doesn't matter whether it's all an elaborate satirical act or if their motivations are sincere. Your *instincts* alone should tell you to avoid following these kinds of toxic personalities. Their brand of dark and jarring humor often contains unspoken truths but shouldn't be seen as anything more than a source of cheap laughs. I have to wonder about the type of person who actually thinks these people are totally legit and takes The Daily Stormer seriously as an authority from which to receive their ideological marching orders.

Since the site's inception, writer Colin Liddell and many others have speculated—often quite humorously—that The Daily Stormer is a disruptive op. I honestly don't know if it is or who's behind it, and I have never really cared. This book is more concerned with exploring possible infiltration from those whom you *wouldn't* immediately suspect of having perfidious intentions.

When you get a chance, take a look at any prominent AltRight, Irony or even WeirdTwitter account and scroll through the list of their followers. Just look at all the thousands of generic shitposting accounts, all using similar profile aesthetics and memed lingo. Page after page of Garfield and groyper and honkler avatars, catboys, catgirls, cowboy hat emojis and every account using variations of the same viral terminology like "cringe," "yikes," "smoothbrane, "NPC, "pawg," grifter," "cope," and "lindy," etc. Most of these terms will seem painfully dated a few months from now if they aren't already. These accounts often specialize in the most pointless and juvenile content imaginable, which consists of almost nothing but stolen jokes and trendy meme lingo. Now I'm not suggesting that *all* or even *most* of these accounts are secretly feds, though some are. The numerical breakdown of those which are real vs. those which are part of an extended network of sockpuppets created to signal-boost memes—is irrelevant. What should be alarming is the *ease* with which a critical mass of people can be programmed into adopting lingo and imagery almost overnight. This process can be organic or directed. Since this process *can* be directed, we must assume that it *is* being directed. If so, then *by whom* and for what purpose? It's safe to assume that— in part—it's being orchestrated by those who have much more resources at their disposal than you or me.

Many years ago, when I was confined to the realm of conventional employment, I interviewed for a position at Yelp. Their interview process consisted of the prospective employee meeting with three different managers separately, one after the other. The first interviewer would make some pleasant introductory small talk, roleplay a sales scenario and then give you critical feedback. The second interviewer would come in and engage in *another* roleplay. Secretly, he/she would be looking to see if you had applied the feedback which was given by the previous manager. The second manager would also give you some feedback. The third and final interviewer would engage in *yet another* roleplaying scenario, this time checking to see if you had incorporated the feedback from the first two managers into your pitch. The purpose was to determine whether the candidate was "coachable" and could be molded into the kind of salesperson who would follow Yelp's assembly line sales system to the letter, without question. Needless to say, I did not get the job.

The extent to which viral meme imagery and lingo are incorporated into someone's social media presence could serve as a litmus test for assessing how easily manipulated or impressionable that person is. A profile that's loaded with this sort of vapid content indicates a person who's highly susceptible to programming, or *perhaps* even someone who's in league with the programmers themselves. Whereas someone who's more reluctant to embrace the latest meme could be seen as having a greater resistance and capable of maintaining a higher degree of independent thought. The process is interesting. "Influencers" and "early adopters" can get others to adopt various fun and innocuous icons, emojis, avatars, lingo, etc. Getting people to embrace these harmless memetic artifacts as part of their online personalities establishes a pattern of social control and softens you up for programming. When it's time for them to sprinkle in some ideological content, you're already used to taking cues from them and will be primed and ready to go along with whatever they have lined up next.

Unfortunately, few of us are completely resistant. I wish I could say that I was totally immune to this form of manipulation, but indeed I have tepidly and at times, enthusiastically been swept up in many memes and diversionary "ops" over the years. It's difficult not to be. People want to be part of something fun. They want to laugh and be entertained. They want to be in on the latest inside jokes and don't want to be left out of the hottest craze. They crave the constant dopamine hits that come with high-engagement social media posts. Authentic dissident political advocacy on the other hand is an isolating and dreary business. Let's face it, it can be depressing. Actually caring about people, pursuing impossible dreams, taking ideas seriously and expressing personal vulnerability are all considered "cringe" in the age we live in. This is to say nothing of the tangible consequences one faces for being a genuine political dissident, consequences which often include social ostracism. You risk getting fired, blacklisted from future employment and disowned by friends and family. You can even be sued into oblivion or arrested on trumped up charges. It's no mystery then that people would find the world of anonymous shitposting and performative irony to be a more attractive domain.

There's a reason Randian individualism fails to ever gain much traction. People are tribal. They seek acceptance, approval and validation from groups. They want to enjoy things and just have a good time, engaging with the world. Few are going to opt for the lifestyle of a reverse **Sour Patch Kid** or some defiantly grumplicious curmudgeon who has walled himself off from popular culture.

A scene from the 1971 post-apocalyptic film *The Omega Man* comes to mind, where mutants voice their frustrations over Charlton Heston's character, Neville, a surviving human they're unable to get to.

> Matthias: One creature, caught. Caught in a place he cannot stir from in the dark, alone, outnumbered hundreds to one, nothing to live for but his memories, nothing to live with but his gadgets, his cars, his guns, gimmicks... and yet the whole family can't bring him down from that, that...
> Zachary: Honky paradise, brother?"
>   - *The Omega Man* (1971)

Perhaps an example of these agents attempting to bring us down and draw us out of our ideological fortifications could be found in the events surrounding the Democratic presidential candidate Andrew Yang's overnight groundswell of support within AltRight (or post-AltRight) circles. A few months ago, when an avalanche of Yang memes seemed to appear out of nowhere, Hunter Wallace pointed out that this wasn't an organic phenomenon and that Yang was clearly getting a "boost" from somewhere. Wallace was certainly correct about that. Yang had been a nobody until that point. It was likely a coordinated op, but conducted by whom? I have some ideas about who was directing it and what the reasons were, though it's all speculation (why should I stop now?).

It's hard to tell to what extent anything that originates from places like 4chan and 8chan is even real anymore. I'm beginning to question to what extent it ever was. Anyhow, Yang's $1000 per month universal basic income or "NEETbux" proposal was an easily meme-able concept, and Yang's candidacy was inflated in what could be described as a "pump and dump" scheme, similar to those used in the seedy world of pinksheets and penny stocks promotion. Bearing that in mind, it's funny how unintentionally appropriate those vaporwave "pink hats" were after all. Let's explore...

What motivation would the feds, or any equivalent entity, have for *astroturfing* in support of Yang's candidacy?

1. The explosion of pro-Yang memes coincided with a time of despair for the fragmented remnants of the AltRight as well as those who had abandoned nationalist activism altogether. People were disillusioned with the broken promises of the Trump presidency, blackpilled and withdrawing from the political process. It's easy to see why this kind of disengaged mindset would be perceived as dangerous or threatening to the establishment. Jaded people who no longer believe in the system are going to be more at risk for committing random acts of political violence and be more receptive to extremist ideologies with revolutionary aims. The Yang memes offered a means to lure these individuals back into investing in electoral politics by making things fun again. For many people, it was a chance to recapture the spirit and "meme magic" they experienced during the 2016 election campaigning for Trump. More importantly though, YangGang offered former AltRight activists a pathway to reestablish themselves in polite society. For young people who've been doxed and/or faced diminished employment and higher educational prospects due to their political views, there develops a sense that their lives are ruined, and they have no hope for the future. Whether or not this is *actually true* doesn't matter. What matters is that if a socially exiled person believes they have nothing to look forward to, like a cornered animal they will be more likely to engage in desperate acts of violence. These creatures need to be brought back into the fold.

Even among those not really at risk for exhibiting violent behavior, many Trump supporters, identitarians and nationalists of varying stripes have been subjected to social alienation as fallout for their politically incorrect opinions. I must admit, this was largely (in addition to his $1000 per month UBI proposal) what attracted me to supporting Andrew Yang, or Tulsi Gabbard for that matter. As someone who has lost many close friends over the last several years due to politics, "YangGang" seemed like a welcome change, an opportunity to engage in a risk-free form of political activism which —for once—wouldn't get me branded a social pariah...

> "Hey man, I heard you're some kind of AltRight neo-nazi now. What's up with that?"
> "Who, me? No way, dude. I'm voting for Andrew Yang."
> "Oh, cool."

Yeah, let's face it. A lot of people were thinking the same thing, including those who were likely responsible for conducting this op.

2. Another possible reason the feds or any similar entity may have had for "boosting" Yang's candidacy could be as an experiment to see the true extent to which memes can influence an election. When Trump ran for president, he was *already* one of the most famous celebrities in the world, someone with a colorful history in

the limelight spanning back several decades. Most Americans had formed some opinion—positive or negative—of Trump prior to his presidential run. It is therefore difficult to gauge the impact AltRight trolls, memes etc. had in affecting the outcome of the 2016 election. Trump won by only a paper-thin margin in several states. It left many wondering, just *how* instrumental were those hordes of RedHat shitposters and Pepe memes in getting him elected? How many licks *did* it take to get to the center of that **Tootsie Roll Pop**? The world may never know. Andrew Yang, on the other hand, had very little name recognition when he announced his bid for president. Hardly anyone had ever heard of him outside the box of Reddit **Nerds** and unironic TED talk enthusiasts, two groups which substantially overlap. Whichever entity was responsible for conducting the Yang op would be therefore working from scratch, allowing them to gain a clear understanding of the degree to which coordinated memetic activism can influence the outcome of "democratic" elections. Amusingly, this experiment seems to have been cut short by the oblivious actions of Yang *himself.* Ever since the people associated with this project jumpstarted his campaign and catapulted him into contention, Yang has cluelessly gone out of his way to alienate his most enthusiastic supporters among the disaffected AltRight and imageboard communities. Not recognizing his most viable base of support—i.e. moderate Democrats who are tired of political correctness, former Trump supporters, post-AltRight nihilists and accelerationists—Yang became just another generic anti-white Democrat, fully embracing the SJW insanity. *All he had to do* was focus on his $1000 a month campaign proposal, take moderate (by today's standards) positions on social issues and not be anti-white. Yang revealed that he wasn't up to it, and most of these early supporters have in turn, slowly abandoned him. Yang's too well known now to be relegated completely back to obscurity. Regarding the aims of this experiment, though, Yang bit into the **Tootsie Roll Pop**, so the world may never know. Sigh.

3. One also cannot rule out the possibility that this op was done strictly for fun and amusement. Monitoring political extremists on 8Chan and Twitter must seem like a tedious chore from time to time. Since they are not passionately invested in the ideas promulgating throughout these circles, we must assume that agents, assets, etc. occasionally behave like slacker employees would at *any other job*. In fact, these feds likely have a lot of discretion and are under very little supervision. Many are probably only in their 20s. They probably spend a lot of time goofing off, crafting pointless projects and writing BS reports to justify whatever they're wasting their time on. Given the positions they're in, they probably feel like they can get away with almost anything. As Richard Nixon once said, *"An arrogance, that's what makes a spy. He puts himself above the law."* I'll leave it for the reader to look up the context of Nixon's conversation. Hint: it involved the discussion of a certain

ethnic group and its disproportionate representation in espionage activities. The bottom line is there's an outside chance the Yang op was initiated by a handful of bored, useless agents who were just dicking around.

Nowhere has the propensity for unprofessionalism been more obvious than within the disturbing interactions which occur when "agents" inject themselves into the fabric of social networks and even people's personal lives under the dubious pretext of "pacification." It is here where we see the line begin to blur between the deradicalization-oriented infiltrator and the more familiar, traditional archetype of the agent provocateur. They get you coming and going!

About five years ago (Christmas Day, December 25, 2014 to be exact), I shared a rather mild yet racially charged essay about "Black Privilege," which I had anonymously written for a now defunct blog, to a Facebook group that dealt with "European interests." Within minutes of sharing the link to the article, I received a random friend request, which I accepted. The guy then messaged me almost immediately. He identified himself as a Klansman and *actually* attempted to recruit me into the KKK. He even used some kind of Klansman greeting which I had to Google when he messaged me because I'm not familiar with that culture, and like most people, I honestly had no idea what he was talking about when he opened with "AYAK." Apparently this is a way of asking "Are You a Klansman?" Even though I hold plenty of politically incorrect views, I of course had no interest in joining an organization as depraved as the KKK, so I politely declined. Though the Facebook account of the guy who messaged me no longer exists, I still have a copy of the original exchange:

Facebook User: AYAK

Me: nope

AKIA...why not you yourself? ever thought about it?

Me: It's just not my thing. I don't really share enough beliefs with them to go "all in."

Facebook User: A respectable answer sir. Fight the good fight as best you know how. No one can ask more than this.

Me: Thanks buddy. Same goes for you

Like most late Gen-Xers, my image of the KKK was shaped by being a teenager in the 1990s and watching episodes of *Jerry Springer*, such as "Thanksgiving with the Klan." I realize that this itself is a subversively tainted perception of the organization, but I probably would never have joined anyway, even if this had been a legit invitation, which I doubt it was. At this point, pretty much everyone who's not a clueless normie knows that the KKK—as it exists today—is nothing but a honeypot organization.

Needless to say, this incident totally creeped me out. Even as naive as I was back then, I suspected this guy was probably a federal law enforcement agent, though now I'm thoroughly convinced. What I found disturbing at the time was that I was using an anonymous Facebook account (which didn't reveal my location) and posting in a European group, yet the guy who contacted me was from my own city. That seemed like a little too much of a coincidence. Within an hour of posting an anonymous, racially charged essay (which was mostly satirical, not relating to violence and not threatening in any way whatsoever) to a Euro Facebook group from my *anonymous* Facebook account, an "agent" from the local area was already all up in my business and working up a case file on me. **Big League Chew** on that for a while.

After I wrote *Beatnik Fascism* in 2016, I had emailed copies to "reactionary" bloggers as well as nationalist types I was mutuals with on Twitter, in the hope of getting some publicity and reviews. One of the people I contacted subsequently attempted to recruit me into Identity Evropa (which has since rebranded as American Identity Movement or A.I.M. for short). I had no idea beforehand that this individual was even a member of that organization. They were just a casual social media acquaintance. I had no substantive reason to suspect this person was a fed, other than that the organization itself has long been suspected of being a honeypot. Still, that doesn't necessarily mean he would have been in on it. He could have just been a rank and file member who genuinely thought I might be a good fit. In any case, I politely declined. I would never join this organization, for a multitude of reasons:

1. I'm not an activist. I have no interest in shouting slogans on the sidewalk, interrupting events at bookstores or putting on Toys"R"Us bought armor and brawling with riff-raff in the streets. I'm a writer. I'm interested in ideas and poetry and inspiration and dreams. I recognize that activists have a role to play, but people should stick to the role that best suits them. Street activism isn't for me.

2. Legal reasons. Being associated with these organizations means that you could potentially be held liable for acts committed by other members of the organization, especially if you ever rise to a leadership role. You could be named in lawsuits. You could become a "fall guy," set up by others to take the blame for their actions. If a member does something insane which results in a shocking news story and subsequent crackdown, you could wind up collateral

damage, being made an example of as part of the government's scorched-earth campaign in response to the public outrage. It doesn't even matter if you are *totally* innocent. We've already seen that the facts don't matter much in these court cases. The trials are politically motivated show trials, and the clueless juries are swayed by emotional arguments. We've seen this time and time again with the preposterous decisions and lopsided sentences in the wake of Charlottesville and numerous other events where street violence has occurred. In 2016, however, when the IE member tried to recruit me, this may not have been as clear of an issue, but it was still on my radar. Even then, I was familiar with the problems Tom and John Metzger had experienced with W.A.R. (White Aryan Resistance) back in the early 1990s, and this has always been in the back of my mind when considering involvement with these types of groups.

3. Perhaps the biggest reasons I would never have joined Identity Evropa were the glaring red flags associated with the organization. The group's founder was Nathan Damigo, a guy who had previously spent a few years in prison for robbing a cab driver at gunpoint. Now, it's very easy for someone who gets released to end up back in prison if they mess up, so many of them go ridiculously out of their way to lead "squeaky clean" lives. You would think Damigo would not start a controversial activist organization which would involve him getting into street fights with people, something

that would surely lead him on a fast track to being thrown back the pen. If I had just been released from prison, I would be staying out of trouble, maybe cleaning swimming pools or planting a garden or something, above all avoiding any activities which could even remotely be perceived as criminal. That's just me. It's also curious that he punched a woman during the Berkeley riots in 2017 but did not appear to face any significant criminal charges, even though it was captured in a video which went viral. Why not? Other "pro-white" activists have received multi-year prison sentences for "assaults" at similar events. Rightly or wrongly, anyone released from prison should be viewed with some skepticism and kept at arm's length. Such a person would have had extensive interactions with law enforcement and potentially been subjected to coercion. It's unfair, but there's no telling what kind of deals a person would have made to escape a desperate situation.

Now, I don't want to come out and say that I think he was a protected informant, because I really have no idea, and that's not where I'm going with this at all. In this instance it doesn't even matter, and here's why. On the Identity Evropa application, they asked if you had visible tattoos, and they also included a question pertaining to criminal history. It makes sense to screen potential members of a political organization, filtering out criminals and overly tatted up freaks in order to build a group which presents to the public a certain clean-cut image. Here's the problem, though.

Since Damigo was in fact a convicted criminal, IE was not in any position to exclude people on that basis. Not only that, but Damigo was a tattoo artist with *visible tattoos* of his own (Davis). So I guess what I'm getting at is that I don't think you should ever join an organization where the leaders don't measure up to the standards they apply when scrutinizing prospective members. In the end, whether or not Identity Evropa was a honeypot is a moot point. The blatant hypocrisy in the screening process was a disqualifying red flag for me and should have been reason enough for anyone to be wary of joining.

I've been hesitant to include specific, documented examples from media sources, because we're quickly approaching an age where we can no longer uncritically believe what we read in news reports, documents or see in videos. The contemporary mainstream media is overtly politicized, plagued with propagandists and riddled with incompetence across the board, yet most "independent" outlets lack the credibility for their claims to be taken seriously by those outside their esoteric spheres of influence. They too suffer from similar problems of bias and low journalistic standards, albeit on a different scale, one where there is pretty much a wild west, "anything goes" attitude toward accuracy. We can no longer take any of this at face value, and many don't, which is why even if you send someone a news article that supports your interpretation of events, they will often dismiss it—regardless of whether it's factual —if it contradicts what they believe and/or comes from a source they perceive to be dubious. Separate news items about the same subject and even scientific studies often totally contradict one another, allowing people to cherry pick "the truth" they wish to accept as real.

And what is the point of citing a news report, photograph or leaked document if six months from now it will turn out to have been fabricated? We have no definitive means to verify the verifiers. With advancements in editing technology and the imminent reality of *Running Man* style "deep fakes," even direct video evidence may no longer be very reliable. Remember a few years ago when MSNBC deceptively doctored the audio of the George Zimmerman 911 call in a way which made Zimmerman appear to bring up Trayvon Martin's race? In the unedited audio, it was clear that *the dispatcher* was the one who asked Zimmerman what Martin's race was, and Zimmerman simply answered the question. MSNBC issued a non-apology calling it an "error" (Bond). Yeah, right. Unfortunately, this trend will only continue.

One of the themes of this book is that we must learn to rely on our own sharpened intuition and heightened perception. It may not be ideal, but we can now only trust what we have *first-hand* experience with. To any information which originates from a third party, we must apply whatever means of scrutiny is available and go with our gut. We must adapt to develop what could be called low level *psychic* powers.

But for those fedora-wearing bugmen who might consider that a *copout* and insist on asking "*Where's the beef?*" I will at least throw you a couple of milkbones:

There was the recent case of the Poway synagogue shooting, which was allegedly committed by a man named John T. Earnest on April 27, 2019. I say "allegedly" only because at the time of this writing the trial hasn't officially concluded. The shooting *incident* itself isn't what's relevant here anyway. During the court proceedings, the "application for a search warrant" document was unsealed. This document included screenshots which revealed that an FBI agent, Michael J Rod (a name which sounds like it's straight out of *Boogie Nights)* had likely been posting in 8Chan threads ("Affidavit In Support of An Application For a Search Warrant" United States v. 8ch.net). The nature of his posts was even more disturbing. He was trying to implicate Russia in a conspiracy theory and divert the posters' focus away from the US government or Mossad. While the court document does not contain *all* of the agent's posts, the original thread is archived and still online.

Here are some excerpts of his posts, which shrewdly attempt to redirect 8chan users' conspiratorial ire toward Russia:

[...I'd blame Mossad, the CIA and FBI too, but this time I am not so sure. We know all three of them can meme because we are shilled all day long by them....]

[This was posted by one of the shills that knew of the shooting prior. Notice screen shot is at 20:00. That correlates with ukraine and western russia if you do the math.]

[Seriously, one of you has to dig on this. Please review this thread. There is some russian/ukranian involvement.]

("Inspired by Tarrant shooting muslims." /pol/ 8Chan)

Notice what he *doesn't* do. He doesn't LARP as a "costume Nazi" or encourage violence to provoke people and make their movement look crazy. He simply attempts to nudge them in a different direction and pacify their hostility toward the US government and its ally, Israel.

The US is *supposedly* prohibited from conducting psyops on its domestic population. However, they've managed to easily get around this by employing euphemisms and legal loopholes to justify their nefarious activities (Elstad). I don't consider myself any kind of law expert, so I don't pretend to know with any certainty what can be characterized as a "psyop" in the strict legal sense and whether the government is *technically* acting illegally or not. In this case, it seems like a distinction rather than a difference. If the government has federal agents posing as political dissidents who post insincere ideological content on widely viewed social media platforms, surely that is going to *influence* the emotions and opinions of the general public. What the *hell* else would you call that but a *psychological* operation?

It is common knowledge that the government has people infiltrating identitarian groups and assuming useful roles within those organizations. Even if such actions are taken under the noble guise of "preventing terrorism," the prominent visibility of movement "thought leaders" virtually guarantees in effect—if not by intent—that the government has people publicly conveying white nationalist talking points to large domestic audiences. If these assets are participating in marches and rallies and chanting slogans in front of cameras, with the resulting footage being broadcast throughout the entire Western world, that is certainly going to influence public opinion. Last but not least, if the feds are indeed running popular irony accounts which farm content and shitpost all day, employing mindless entertainment as a means of mitigating radicalism and numbing the dissident community to the point where they no longer give a rat's ass about anything, then yeah, that is probably going to have a psychological effect on a substantial segment of the American population.

Another example of sub-ethical use of intelligence resources can be found in the case surrounding Jerry Drake Varnell, a young Oklahoma man recently convicted of plotting to blow up a BancFirst building back in 2017:

> Varnell, 23, was arrested without incident in the early morning hours of Aug. 12 after he allegedly called a cell phone number he thought would detonate a bomb in a truck parked behind the BancFirst building, 101 N Broadway. The person who assisted him with building the bomb was working for the FBI, and the device was inert. (Wingerter)

At first glance it all seems like a pretty straightforward and properly executed sting operation. Once again, however, when the details come to light they reveal a different picture. It turns out that Jerry Drake Varnell was a schizophrenic with a long history of mental illness.

The FBI used an informant named Brent Elisens who had a criminal record and *also* suffered from mental health issues:

> He said he has been hospitalized at least three times
> for post-traumatic stress disorder and other mental
> health problems, and he was sentenced to 30 months
> in prison in 2011 after pleading guilty to calling in a
> bomb threat to the Norman Police Department.
>
> (Wingerter)

It's already troubling enough that the FBI would trust *and pay* over $23,000 to someone with this kind of unstable background to carry out a sensitive sting operation relating to something as serious as domestic terrorism. What's even worse though is that the FBI informant appeared not only to instigate but *aggressively encourage* the highly impressionable Varnell to commit an attack. Throughout their correspondence, Varnell seemed *barely* interested, often giving brief, passive responses to the FBI informant's pushy suggestions, while other times ignoring them completely and not responding at all. I don't have access to the original transcripts, so I can only reference the portion which appeared in a Ramzpaul video that dealt with this story. Basically though, Varnell's words seemed in line with what one would say when trying to avoid someone by being short with them, with answers like "OK" and "Sounds good."

8/3/2017 Elizens: Hey man what's the story with the vehicles and containers?

Varnell: [no response]

8/4/2017 Elizens: Hey man we should probably talk sometime soon about next week. I can call you tomorrow if you're around.

8/4/2017 Varnell: I'm going to be building fence all day tomorrow

8/6/2017 Elizens: I'm going to call you tomorrow and talk about the schedule

8/6/2017 Varnell: ok

8/7/2017 Elizens: [attempted call, no answer]

8/7/2017 Varnell: Showering call you back in 20 [never called]

8/8/2017 Elizens: I'm in between something but call when you can. If I cannot answer will call u asap

8/8/2017 Varnell: [no response]

8/8/2017 Elizens: Let me know when you can talk

8/8/2017 Varnell: [no response]

("Criminalizing Mental Illness," Ramzpaul)

As you can see, Jerry Drake Varnell seemed *less than enthusiastic* about participating in this terror plot (the plans for which seem to have been drawn up by the FBI themselves.) There's no question that Varnell represents a danger to society and himself. We know this since he ultimately agreed to proceed with what he believed was a bomb attack. The issue is that the FBI targeted someone who was mentally ill and tried to push him into acting on his most monstrous inclinations, just so they could get a scalp. At the first sign of Varnell's willingness to engage in violence, the FBI could have worked to get him help, perhaps by showing his parents the evidence and convincing them to commit him to a mental institution. The feds demonstrated questionable judgment at best, while at worst their actions could be characterized as grossly negligent and perversely sadistic. It was all so unnecessary. Varnell is by no means innocent, but he wasn't the only malefactor in this saga. Just the one with the least amount of agency.

This manipulation of "test" subjects isn't limited to Hollywood archetypal provocateurs seeking to coax mentally ill people into incriminating themselves in deranged terror plots. The practice also seems to be commonly employed by deradicalization and misdirection agents who are targeting dissidents, though their precise motivations may be murky.

It may be used for surveillance purposes, to build a control file on someone or get a foothold within dissident social groups in order to gain their trust, with these agents finagling their way into a position where they can monitor and influence activities to a greater degree, as part of "the long game" of impeding the development of dissident movements. They may be studying your reactions to various stimuli, gauging your response to the many modes of poking, probing and prodding they use to provoke you. They gather this data not just to determine your weaknesses but to get a broader understanding of dissident personalities in general. It's not all that different from standard animal testing. For example: a group of lab rats might be used for a specific scientific study, but the resulting information is documented and may be relevant to other studies, or prove useful in some future, totally unrelated application.

Some agents have a unique way of communicating on social platforms, one that is actually quite clever. Instead of talking directly via DM (direct message) or in a threaded conversation, they post a message on their own timeline from a low-follower locked account. The other person responds by posting on his/her own respective timeline. Usually only one of the accounts will be viewable to the general public. Unlike with DMs or group chats, which can be screenshotted and leaked *in their entirety*, this method is not traceable because the communication is not addressed to anyone in a *documentable* format. The agents talk back and forth without ever directly "@ing" one another. In a compromised situation, a curious observer will likely never have access to anything but an incomplete (and probably useless) portion of the conversation. One could correctly ascertain what the other party might be saying by analyzing a piece of the dialogue, but in such a case the agents will have still left themselves room for deniability. Amusingly, this effective communication method is *also* often used by people in relationships who are attempting to conceal flirtatiously suggestive communications from their significant other, (who may have access to and be monitoring their private messages.) It's anybody's guess as to which of these groups pioneered this form of communication, feds or adulterers, since there's a lot of overlap and both are often woven *from the same cloth.*

Speaking of which, a componential contributor to this blurred boundary is the psychological interchangeability which agents, informants and various shills share with the subjects whom they've been tasked to surveil and subvert. As acclaimed director William Friedkin once mentioned in an featurette interview concerning the film, *To Live and Die in LA*, "I have found that the nature of cops and criminals is very similar. They understand each other's lingo as though they're brethren, and even the good cops are guys who are walking a very fine line most of the time" (*Counterfeit World: Making 'To Live and Die in L.A,'* Video 2003). For those unfamiliar, the protagonist in To Live and Die in LA is an unscrupulous secret service agent who resorts to illegal and unethical methods to catch a prominent counterfeiter.

"I thought *To Live and Die in LA* was, in all, about a counterfeit world: counterfeit emotions, counterfeit money, counterfeit superstructure of the secret service...Everyone in the film has a kind of counterfeit motive, so it seemed to me that the whole film was about counterfeit relations." -William Friedkin (Counterfeit...)

For those who might scoff at my referencing an 80s "action movie" to illustrate a point, *To Live and Die in LA* was actually based on a novel by Gerald Petievich, a former US secret service agent who served from 1970-1985 and whose novels were known for their authentic portrayals of the job. Of course, when we're talking about political dissidents (even radicals) we're not typically talking about actual criminals, but the dynamic remains the same. Such "thought criminal" figures are perceived as potential threats to the established societal order, just as if they were bank robbers or common hoodlums. They are observed with cynical suspicion (the default setting of many in law enforcement) and treated as though they are loose cannons who could morph into revolutionary terrorists at any moment.

Among those with so called "extremist" views, few political dissidents are physically dangerous or harbor any intention of committing violence. I'm inclined to believe that much of the "monitoring" and needlessly invasive intrusion into people's personal lives amounts to little more than "make work" tasks for agents to justify being paid to do nothing but spend 20 hours a day dicking around on Twitter posting farmed political content and stolen shitty jokes from vintage Tumblr pages. In a recent discussion with my ex-girlfriend, when I brought up the prospect of being monitored, she laughed and responded,
"You once sent me a picture of a dolphin fucking a lady. Whoever is monitoring you is probably sick of you." [Please note that the image she was referring to was from an anime cartoon meme. I don't condone animal cruelty.]

On some level, many of these agents may actually be sympathetic to the beliefs of groups they've infiltrated, though we have no way of knowing to what degree, and since their loyalties are inherently compromised, we can't trust them enough to believe anything they would have to say about it. Some agents may be trying to have their cake and eat it too. They figure they can perform a balancing act where they get paid to express what are mostly their honestly held right-wing opinions, while tweaking them at the margins to steer people away from antisocial behavior and anti-American sentiment. As I've mentioned, feds are after all government employees doing a job and collecting a paycheck. Some probably take their jobs too seriously, while others aren't very motivated or invested in what they're doing. I don't know about your experience, but I've worked a lot of jobs in sales and retail where I've had to sell worthless products I didn't believe were particularly useful, yet I sold them because I had to eat and pay rent. In the late 90s, I worked in a telemarketing call center, and one of the things we sold was a bizarre "utility insurance" plan which would guarantee that if you died your power bill would be paid. People *actually* bought that.

The manipulative intrusion into people's personal relationships though is profoundly disturbing because it represents a violation of one's sense of reality. We expect the shameless exploitation of troubled young women and men by sleazy porn producers and cheap hustlers, but the subjects in those cases are usually at least aware of what they are engaging in and consent to it, even if they are misled about what to expect. The idea of the feds using their own citizens in this manner evokes a special kind of *Twilight Zone* horror. Naively perhaps, we expect our agents to conduct themselves with a minimal standard of integrity, not to use Charles Mansonesque manipulation tactics to push emotionally distraught individuals into pointless liaisons. They torment these people and for what?

THE RAT MEAT MARKET (AN INTERLUDE)

Perhaps some of these agents have stared into the abyss too long and absorbed a glob of the madness so prevalent in the toxic communities they've been assigned to monitor. Some clearly suffer from *severe* mental illness, often abusing their authority and developing inappropriate fixations on well meaning people who are just trying to get their lives together and break out of their troubled past. Instead of trying to *help* these tortured souls, these agents actively torment and take advantage of them, viewing them as pawns to be deployed in any number of their tedious "make work" projects. The result is that people who already struggled with "trust issues" become even more paranoid and reluctant to form healthy relationships.

I'm of course hinting at the way they utilize girls to get to you. "Why not?" a friend jokingly remarked to me. "It only works 100% of the time!" Some of these girls may be working with the feds directly or may even be agents themselves. Others are just unwitting participants manipulated psychologically into interacting with someone who's been identified as a juicy target. There are practically an unlimited number of "wounded" girls on the internet. Using various coordinated psychological techniques, agents can nudge romantically *intrigued* parties toward one another.

Whatever you choose to call them, these glow-in-the-dark matchmakers, pervatronic puppeteers, social-interaction curators and butchers of the rat meat market are a depraved bunch. Admittedly though, despite the insincerity of their intentions, these orchestrated couplings are the deradicalization approach I *personally* find the least objectionable. If the feds want to go through the trouble of supplying me with a stream of troubled e-girls to disrupt my life and make me delightfully miserable so that they may document my nauseatingly personal romantic interactions for their control file, all I can say is that these guys must have a soft spot for me, because that *sure as hell* beats entrapment and spending 20 years in the pokey on some bogus, trumped up "incitement" or "conspiracy" charge. Yes, by all means continue to send me attractive, intelligent girls who fall *precisely* within my target demographic. I'm fairly picky, though, so don't expect me to bite consistently. Over a span of nearly a decade inhabiting nationalist political circles on social media, I have only encountered one e-girl I considered interesting enough to *actually* meet up with, and even then I put in almost zero effort to make it happen. If the purpose is to open me up for a surveillance warrants and track my movements, that would seem a poor use of government resources, unless you believe that watching me go to TJ Maxx and Steinmart every day to look at the discount watches is a matter of national security.

Broke: Meeting generic, "full time dog moms" on Tinder who love hiking and Harry Potter, girls who end up being bots or girls whose accounts exist solely to attempt to scam you into giving them money.

Woke: Edgeposting for years online, firmly establishing yourself as a prominent political dissident and waiting for the feds to set you up with a highly desirable, intellectually stimulating and romantically compatible female companion as part of an ethically questionable, labyrinthine psychological study and depraved deradicalization campaign (paid for with boomer tax dollars.)

After all, getting romantically involved with a girl who's been assigned—with or without her knowledge—to spy on you is just another relationship obstacle, a challenge for the Faustian will to overcome. There's going to be some kind of bullshit to deal with in any courtship. Let's face it, you could do *a lot worse* than a fed honeypot gf. I *have* done much worse. I've dated *multiple* hairstylists in my lifetime and have the *thousand yard stare* to prove it. For their part, the female psyop subjects could do a lot worse than a trustworthy guy who's earned his red wings. Well, I'll just leave it at that.

Filmed in Francoist Spain, the 1967 film *Fathom* stars Raquel Welch as Fathom Harvill, a beautiful yet otherwise ordinary member of a US skydiving team that's touring Europe. Under false pretenses, Fathom is coerced by various "agents," thieves, private detectives and other underworld figures into locating and recovering a valuable Chinese artifact known as the "Fire Dragon." None of the shady individuals vying to enlist Fathom's assistance are completely truthful about who they are or the honorability of their intentions, and she finds herself being used as a pawn by nearly every side. Caught smack-dab in the middle of this high stakes, calamitous caper, the confused Fathom struggles to determine whom she can trust, while occasionally managing to turn the tables on her manipulators by employing some clever schemes of her own.

I've probably seen the movie *Fathom* more than 200 times over the years. It has always been my first choice if I was hanging out with a girl I really liked and had to pick out something for us to watch, but the vast majority of times I've seen it have been when I was drinking alone in my living room, just blurting out lines of dialogue I had memorized and vibing out to the underrated soundtrack. Now when I re-watch the film—which I have been doing every day since I began writing this book—*Fathom* causes me to reflect on all these "Fedfish" bait girls, and I try to imagine how they ever managed to get mixed up in any of this in the first place. What percentage of these temptresses are like Fathom Harvill, good-natured young women who were merely thrust into these situations unwittingly, *misguided* girls who just happened to land in the wrong place at the wrong time?

What percentage are cold-hearted succubus shrews, more closely resembling Elke Sommer and Sylva Koscina's cunning and cruel duo in *Deadlier Than the Male?* Which one are you?

There have been colossal tomes written about the mind control methods used by military intelligence, weird cults and other serial abusers. If you decide to take the Nestea® Plunge and delve into these books and documents, I'd recommend that you *also* take much of what is written with a grain of salt. Subjects like MKultra and "Project Monarch" manage to bring a lot of batshit crazy people out of the woodwork, which is why "normal" people just roll their eyes when anyone brings this stuff up. It's a special kind of hell to be minding your own business at a party, quietly enjoying a *Stella Artois* and scoping out the scene for vivacious young women, when out of nowhere some drunken crackpot corners you and starts blathering on incessantly about the high crimes of the illuminati.

In any 1000 page compendium devoted to these issues, you will encounter more than your fair share of utter nonsense. If you have the patience to slog through it, try to analyze each individual claim on its own and ask yourself "Does this seem *plausible* ?" "Does it make *sense?*" Eccentric conspiracists can occasionally unearth eye-opening tidbits, even if the conclusions drawn from them constitute an unjustified leap.

One thing I *can* say is that even if the government no longer operates these programs in any official capacity, the "mind control" techniques which emerged from the experiments continue to be studied and used by agents when it suits their aims. (It's not as if doctors just threw away the treasure trove of knowledge obtained from unethical medical experiments conducted by the Soviet Union, Germany and the USA during the 20th century.) Even if you were to remove the government conspiracy angle from the equation, there is widespread—and possibly more credible— literature available on the methods used by cults to brainwash people, as recounted by survivors and former members through testimony. A person or group need not be acting on behalf of some hypothetical "new world order" cabal to adopt these methods. The techniques can be incorporated into any resourceful huckster's two-bit street scams or applied by any pimp who's just trying to a few uppity hoes in line.

Many of the traditional techniques associated with programming a subject involve forms of *physical* torture and trauma, most of which would require extensive in-person interaction and don't seem like they would be applicable to social media oriented ops. However, the internet makes it easy for agents to identify and select "ideal" candidates who—through their online behavior—show signs of having *already* experienced emotional trauma or physical abuse in their lives. These people come primed, shrinkwrapped and ready for handling. The *hard* work has already been done for the agents. There is no shortage of "traumatized" women (and men) active on social media. One common thread that runs through all the mind control "literature" is that programmers seek out subjects who have dissociative disorders. Supposedly, "mental dissociation enables the handlers to create walled-off personas in the subject's psyche, which can then be programmed and triggered at will" (Vigilant Citizen, 2012).

Now, we're getting into something I've actually seen put into practice. They will send the subject certain trigger phrases or images, perhaps a photograph of an object or of *someone*, and you can witness in real time how the subject's personality completely changes in the blink of an eye. At first it just comes off like you're dealing with a scatterbrained or airheaded individual, but over time —if you're paying attention and making mental notes—you'll notice there's a *repetitive pattern* to the circumstances in which it happens. It's very disturbing to see this occur first hand. The person's tone changes from one moment to the next (if you're on the phone, even their *voice* can change). Their statements seem disconnected from one another other (and from reality), to the point where—and this is key—you wonder if they are mistaking you for *someone else.*

Skimming through the laundry list of alleged physical and psychological torture methods used for programming, one item in particular jumped out at me:

30. Use of illusion and virtual reality to confuse and create non-credible disclosure. (Lacter)

This is one I have some personal familiarity with. The goal here is to confuse the subject, create stress and lead them to question their sense of reality, ultimately causing them to dissociate. An example would be if agents were to create multiple accounts pretending to be a specific person and then have those accounts attempt to interact with the subject. The tedious cycle of ceaselessly creating new accounts and circumventing subsequent blocks would quickly induce frustration. The messages themselves could contain triggers and build a framework for whatever the long game is (which probably involves targeting the individual they're impersonating).

There are so many ways to harass someone or mess with their head online, I couldn't even begin to list them all.

The last part about "creating non-credible disclosure" relates to what I talked about earlier in the book. They bombard the subject with minor illusions, with the cumulative effect being that the subject begins to act out in ways that seem paranoid and delusional to others. Then, when the subject attempts to reveal what's being done to them and what activities they're involved in, *no one will believe them*, since the truth will be mixed with easily verifiable falsehoods and explainable coincidences. I believe this is one reason people have such a hard time breaking their conditioning. Doctors are of limited help because they will detect the obvious inaccuracies and will assume the subject is mistaken about *everything else* as well. The doctor will then focus on treating things from a "paranoia" angle, rather than a deprogramming approach. I don't believe that most doctors—for moment than a brief moment—seriously entertain the remote possibility that their patient *really was* psychologically manipulated by government agents.

It may be worthwhile to inquire whether that girl you're enjoying a passionate flirtation with online has ever been diagnosed with any type of dissociative identity disorder. If indeed she has, that could indicate she's being used by someone else to get close to you. (I'll leave it to the reader to come up with a tactful way to work this into casual conversation.) You may be able to learn everything you need to know just by observing though.

As I write this, I ask myself why I bother even trying to counter these actors. Can one sensitive cancerian 80's kid armed with nothing but his wits and an overly active imagination manage to derail the subversive machinations of embedded legions of cunning and ruthless fratbro agents backed by the full might of an (albeit fading) imperial bureaucratic juggernaut? To quote Michael in that iconic motorcycle chase scene from *The Lost Boys*, *"I can't beat your bike."*

And yet, I Still Believe.

THE RATS OF NATIONALISM (CONTINUED)

Once you begin to identify a few of the prominent actors on social media who are involved in deradicalization measures and coordinated efforts to (mis)manage public opinion on social media, the picture becomes clearer and patterns start to reveal themselves.

Every morning, like clockwork, you will see these accounts all on the same page, participating in the same threads, pushing the same memes and amplifying subtly different versions of the same talking points. After a while, when you see a new account has been created, you'll be able to correctly guess which accounts it follows just by looking at it. Watch for yourself. Notice who the major players are, and observe the cycle repeat itself day in and day out. I promise you, when you see one of these people promoting a particular line you'll be able to predict which others will be in on the action.

Recently I came across several recently created trad "girl" accounts, each of which had a similar appearance and posting style, as if they were working from a template or according to a proven formula. I pointed these accounts out to a friend, and he agreed that they all appeared to be "different permutations of the same person." *What are they up to?* I wondered. To quote a popular song by The Hollies, *"Hey Carrie Anne, what's your game now, can anybody play?"* The cookie-cutter assortment of motifs associated with this particular brand of suspicious accounts is so familiar to me by now that it stands out like a striped-shirted Waldo on the beach.

How do I presume to know about all this or *any* of this? Maybe I'm just highly intuitive and excel at pattern recognition. Or, perhaps I got a tip from someone. Maybe a wounded blue jay whispered a secret in my ear one evening before flying away capriciously in the early morning. Or, who knows? Maybe I just casually asked my glow-in-the-dark Ouija board just who or what else glows in the dark, and it gave me an answer which contained more information than my soul could bargain for. Maybe a certain percentage of this book is just me thinking out loud and talking out of my ass, while the remaining percentage involves me relaying things I know for a fact. I won't reveal the exact numerical breakdown because I'm not entirely sure myself, and I hate math. *Math is a movie ruiner.* It has a way of needlessly complicating dreams.

POST-RAT NATIONALISM

"You won't believe this, but I don't enjoy throwing you back to the lions.

...

On the other hand, it's the only way you'll discover I'm the good guy in this story. Suddenly I can't think of anything more important."

        - Peter Merriwether, Fathom, 1967

By now you might be wondering whether this is all just an exercise of pissing in the pool or if I actually have any practical solutions to offer. I hate to disappoint you, but the reality is that not much can be done. These infiltrators are so *widely* dispersed, so *deeply* embedded and have done *so much* damage already that it's almost pointless to attempt to weed them out at this stage. I'm not sure how you would even begin. Once you start down the road of naming names and publicly calling out specific people as being "feds," you can very quickly gain a reputation as "*that guy,*" like so many insufferable forum kooks and grouchy old YouTube personalities who accuse *practically everyone* of being a shill or "controlled opposition." The government would like nothing more than for things to devolve into a total shitshow where everyone takes turns angrily accusing one another of being feds. The feds have already pre-emptively and successfully spread the meme of ironically self-identifying as a fed anyway. It's practically everywhere. Look around, and you will notice hundreds if not thousands of accounts jokingly incorporating "fed" into a clever username or bio and making it just another goofy facet of their online persona. Therefore, even the most persuasive and fervent attempts to publicly expose an agent will be met not with denials but with laughter and mockery. "Yeah guys, he's right! This big brained nibba has my number. Of course I'm a fed. You are all under arrest! lmoa." They will have an army of both real and figurative sockpuppet acolytes to back them up and "ratio" you. People have already been programmed not to take anything that matters seriously. Being real is "cringe." Caring about politics is "cringe." Love is "cringe." Hate is "cringe." All emotions are "cringe." Anything except for ironically identifying as a fed is either "cringe" or "a cope."

Aside from the fact that I always hated the movie *The Matrix*, one reason I've never cared much the red pill/blue pill analogy is that I've always identified more with the color blue. Blue traditionally represents sincerity, intuition, imagination, nostalgia, sensitivity, wisdom and loyalty – all valuable characteristics which seem to be lacking (with the exception of nostalgia) in dissident political movements, especially among those who claim to be "redpilled." Regardless of what they're going for, most of these "red pill" types come off as arrogant, impulsive, unimaginative, crude and dumb, though I will concede that a handful are charismatic and passionate.

Of course, the inherent dynamism of online culture permits nearly infinite rebranding, which can be coordinated and implemented at the drop of a hat. So even if we were to encourage people to avoid performative irony and instead embrace qualities like sincerity and authenticity, the feds could easily subvert this by formulating a "genuineness" meme, and overnight their hordes of accounts would be turning over a new leaf and converting to phony "seriousposting" accounts en masse. They already have plenty of accounts like this anyway, as part of their "balancing act." I could easily envision a scenario where these people jokingly change their avatars to cartoon rats and other characters from *The Secret of NIMH* upon the release of this book just to mock it. Suddenly "Smurf Nationalism" is everywhere, and profiles are given a fresh coat of paint to the tune of The Fleetwood's *Mister Blue* (or Eiffel 65's *Blue* if you prefer).

One novel solution might be to just aggressively play along. This would consist of latching on to each newly orchestrated e-trend, co-opting it for the purpose of boosting your own popularity and increasing your influence. Maybe farm *their* content for a change. Once you or your group have managed to siphon enough clout by pushing these shitty memes to the max, you can pivot toward *your own* sincere ideas, taking the loyal following you've built with you. This is almost a mirror image of what infiltrators do to you. Incidentally (or so we assume), it's *also* what people like Milo and Cernovich and Roosh seem to have done successfully for so many years: glob on to a new trend and use it as a vessel to advance their own ideological niches, pet projects and personal brand. Nothing new really. There are problems with this approach, though. For one thing, we need to attract people of substance, and such people are generally put off by behaviors that appear unprincipled and opportunistic. You'll appear untrustworthy. After all, no one but you and a handful of close confidantes will know that your true intentions are noble. Everyone else will think you're just another huckster. Trust is such a rare and indispensable commodity within these circles, that I'm not sure it's worth sacrificing for anything (well, almost anything). The other issue with attempting to repurpose other people's ops is that you'll never really be sure if *you're* using them or *they're* using you. Who's getting the better end of the deal, and who's getting the shit end of the stick? You may only end up fooling yourself.

Another frequently proposed idea is to move beyond anonymity altogether. Anonymous imageboards like 4chan and 8chan are overrun with shills and bad actors. Not only are they compromised to a state of unusability, they attract the scum of the Earth and foster a climate that's pure poison. It's probably useless to recommend avoiding these boards, though, because—like anything else—impressionable young people just *will not heed sound advice.* They are hopelessly attracted to gutter gossip and vile political content. They can't get enough of it! People will continue to congregate on these sites and fall for the *same tricks* over and over.

Anonymity in general on social media seems to have largely outlived its usefulness. The obvious value in being anonymous is that people can express their true opinions without being fired from their jobs or socially ostracized from family and friends. There are trade-offs, however. Anyone can pretend to be whomever or *whatever* they want. Enemies and subverters have figured this out (it wouldn't take a genius) and have adapted to where they can easily infiltrate political social circles and start posting on behalf of any movement they claim to be a part of. Since their backgrounds are not available for scrutiny, there is no way to know their intentions or assess the validity of their claims or even be able to tell if they are completely full of shit in how they present themselves. There was a popular AltRight figure named Spectre who claimed to be a psychiatrist. I even remember an episode of *Fash the Nation* where he was providing medical analysis of Rubio's dry-mouth problems during one of the 2015-2016 GOP debates. Well, it turned out Spectre was not a doctor of any kind. When he was doxed and his identity was revealed, he turned out to be a journalist from Dallas. You literally have *no idea* who anonymous people are or what they could be concealing about their background.

I find it rather amusing every time I witness some anonymous person lecturing about "soyboys" and "the weakness of modern man" when they themselves don't even have the balls to look someone in the eye and state an opinion.

> *Ancient men conquered cities and put them to the sword and fire, while internet anons lack the courage to publicly express an opinion, terrified that some middle aged woman named Nancy in HR might give them a timeout.*

People should at least get off their high horses with all the talk of steel swords and sunbathing centaurs until they've worked up the courage to tweet something controversial under their own names. If we live in "clown world," why do these people even care so much if they become ostracized from a bunch of *clowns* anyway? Just make some killer balloon animals and have a laugh. Seriously though, "clown world" is merely an outpost that exists under the dominion of a greater "Scam World." That's the world we *truly* inhabit, a world where everyone's trying to put one over on each other in some way. *Even the clowns are working an angle.*

Having said all that, I *don't* encourage people to give up their anonymity. Anyone who aggressively attempts to convince people to self-dox will be viewed with suspicion and rightly so.

Most people are not mentally prepared for the consequences of being doxed or being open about their views. When such types face a few setbacks and are *broken* by the pressure of the system, rather than shrug it off and push forward they tend to lash out and scapegoat those whom they perceive as having "seduced" them into embracing these edgy beliefs in the first place. Note that these are often the *same* people who claim that modern men are weak, effeminate soyboys who refuse to take on adult responsibilities. Yet, when these grown adults—*often in their mid to late 20s*—get doxed and fired because *they* made the conscious decision to attend a *public* political rally, they typically fold like cheap suits and start pointing fingers. No, I don't recommend giving up anonymity. It's a bad idea and will cause *a lot* of problems for you and possibly others who trust you. However, if you are going to be anonymously involved in nationalist politics online for any extended period, you should still always operate under the assumption you *will* inevitably be doxed at some point and forced to answer for everything you have ever have said/posted. If you're not ready to live with the possibility that you may have to publicly stand behind your opinions at an inconvenient time in your life, just don't bother getting involved more than superficially.

Someone once said that the arts are for the independently wealthy and those who are able to just scrape by. The same could be said for dissident politics. If you have enough money and resources to where you can absorb the social punishments and financial pressures imposed for expressing controversial views, then maybe it's *okay* to be open about your beliefs. Similarly, if you're a minimalist who is comfortable scrounging through life with few responsibilities and little to lose, then maybe you can get away with using your real name. Middle-class people with families, however, who would be at risk for losing their houses if they got fired and missed a few mortgage payments, should really limit their involvement in edgy politics to a bare minimum. The same goes for young college students who will be entering the job market and may not even be sure yet of who they are and what they actually believe. I have seen *so many* of these young people come and go over the years. They emerge out of nowhere and go "gung ho" into these movements, enthusiastically joining groups and showing up to events. They're just *so eager* to be involved in everything...

Then six months later they're disavowing everyone, doxing their former friends and leaking chat logs and DMs. Some are probably shills, but *the point* is it's better to wait until you've figured yourself out before potentially branding yourself unemployable for views you *may not even hold* a year or two from now.

The bottom line here is that going public with your views has to be *your* choice, *yours* alone and one *you're* willing to live with forever. Right now (in the US) people just face social and financial consequences for expressing their opinions. We are only one or two election cycles away from being imprisoned for our views under dubious legal pretenses. For some unlucky people, this has begun already. People shouldn't choose this path and many won't, so political circles will continue to be plagued by these kinds of "no barrier to entry" infiltration problems for the foreseeable future.

Getting rid of anonymity wouldn't solve these issues anyway, for another reason. While absolutely any two-bit mischief maker can easily infiltrate an anonymous political "movement," *public* movements are also susceptible to subversion and in ways which the feds have definite advantages. Feds have no trouble being public, because they're well funded and don't have to deal with the looming prospect of losing their jobs. They don't have to worry about being shut down by payment processors or having their bank accounts closed. Without having to worry about maintaining streams of income, they can focus completely on elevating their influence within these movements. It's easy for them to appear confident, well groomed, and comfortable because they know they're *being taken care of*, and an impressive well-funded presentation allows them to easily establish credibility and attract a huge following. Can a broke guy with a camera compete for control of the narrative with a fully financed studio operation? Maybe, but either way it's a challenge that distracts from more productive uses of one's time and resources. While a public figure's background is at least theoretically accessible for scrutiny, the feds have ways of falsifying background info as well as selecting people who would be able to pass through any vetting processes. Once *they* are in position to be the ones doing the vetting, the dilemma compounds itself. Whether anonymous or public, these manipulators always seem to have the upper hand.

Nixon's observation that arrogance is "what makes a spy" may have been correct, but arrogant people have a weakness. They are prone to overestimating themselves and underestimating their opponents. They get cocky and let things slip. They get sloppy and begin to make careless mistakes. Arrogance is often a compensatory posture which masks a deeper insecurity that will reveal itself from time to time. If these moments can be exploited, the entire facade will collapse like a house of cards.

Perhaps a silver lining in all this is that sooner or later the feds will begin to realize they are defending a disintegrating empire from the *only* people still invested in holding any semblance of it together. As it stands, the United States exists as a nation *in name only*, like so many once iconic brands like "Sylvania" and "RCA" whose trademarks have long ago been gobbled up by multinational corporations, to be repurposed. Occasionally these "logos" are then slapped on cheap Chinese electronics in order to market products under a name American consumers associate with quality. If current trends continue, the United States itself will meet the same fate (it may already be too late). If the forces opposed to nationalism continue to have their way, the *very concept* of the "nation state" will be in its death throes. The feds then are essentially working on behalf of a soon to be *non-existent* entity. Without a clearly defined country with established boundaries, what jurisdiction is the US government even presiding over? All that the agencies tasked with administrating these ops are preserving is a giant, third-world international airport that's merely branded with an American flag. At the end of the day, all these online cloak-and-dagger shenanigans amount to is a game of memetic charades on the deck of a pixelated Titanic. Some of these agents *have* to realize this. Nearly everyone has worked a job where they've had to dishonestly defend a product which didn't live up to the brand's reputation. I'm sure this particular "job" pays quite well and is a real dopamine-generator, but your deradicalization efforts are undertaken at the behest of of a borderless country that is 20 trillion dollars in debt and soon to be governed by people who are openly hostile to the ideas of the founders and have nothing but *contempt* for the nation your ancestors built. So, maybe cut those of us who actually care about the future some slack. If not it's cool.

As far as the "MKUltra-lite" girls are concerned, it's unrealistic to advise guys to stay away from e-girls. It will simply *never happen.* Despite the "thot patrol" rhetoric and a relentless barrage of misogynist content, guys have ignored this advice on social media for many years and will continue to interact with these women, because it is fun. They'll continue to be baited into the same catfish routines and suckered into the same honeypot schemes. One thing I *will* recommend, though, is that you increase your awareness, *especially* if you are talking to girls in the nationalist or political dissident community. At least have some idea of the nature of the trap you're walking into when you ignore the red flags and move right in anyway. Life is about taking chances, but be perceptive. If a girl online is behaving in ways which don't conform to what you'd recognize as normal female behavior, if she DMs you out of the blue and starts showing intense romantic interest in you for *no discernible reason,* chances are the interaction may not be on the up and up. Likewise, stop and ask yourself how likely it is that a nubile young woman who resembles a typical sorority thot would spend all day online tweeting about the Jews and posting photographs of ancient European statues? If you meet one of these girls online who's fantastically attractive and miraculously seems to share your socially ostracizing political beliefs and "trad" values *and* also claims to be spellbound by you even though you've never done anything but reply to a couple of her posts, it's safe to assume that something's amiss. If you're lucky, the best case scenario is that she's real but a bit of a **fruit loop**. If you've read this far, you probably have some idea of what the worst case scenarios are. *Don't ever take an e-girl at avatar value*, and be prepared to analyze other content patterns as well, while you're eagerly psyching yourself into believing that this time, it's REAL.

So what *do* I recommend? Anything which could conceivably disrupt efforts at psychological conditioning. I think people need to resist the impulse to base their content around reacting to every viral news item or current event. News stories are often seeded into the public consciousness for a reason, and by devoting your energy to offering commentary on every sensational news headline—regardless of how brilliant and insightful your hot take is—you're still merely participating within a conversational framework that's been dictated by someone else. You're limiting yourself to a range of topics that have been selected by those who are in a position to amplify whatever issues they want people discussing and thinking about. Instead of being drawn into this molasses swamp of thought framing, you should focus on your own ideas and interests. The downside is that almost everyone else will be salivating over the shiny red **gummy bear** that's being dangled in front of their faces every morning. They'll be getting their daily fix of **candy cigs** and won't give a rat's ass in a room full of cats about the random tangent you're off on. That's okay, though. Some people will be curious, and even if they only pay attention a little, you'll have helped them put a dent in *their* conditioning. There are already people who do the news reaction angle quite well anyway. If you're capable of diving deeper into ideas and emotions, you should do that. Don't sell yourself short by getting bogged down in the "outrage porn"-of-the-day.

Anything you can do to sharpen your intuition and enhance your perception is worthwhile. Focus on meditation. Read books on developing psionic abilities and ESP. Practice remote viewing, telepathy, telekinesis, whatever. It doesn't even matter if 99% of it is *complete bullshit*. Anything which potentially alters your way of thinking in ways which inspire you to uncover possibilities, ideas and options other than those laid out in front of you every day may prove useful in circumventing psychological subversion.

One remote but recurring thought that has crossed my mind is that perhaps I've been targeted precisely because they wanted me to write this book. That somehow based on my psychological profile it was evident that I would react in *just this manner*, and this entire literary exercise is in line with the aims of some broader mindfuck experiment. If true, all I can do is wink back at the observers, and take comfort in the realization that at least my power level of *awareness* is growing.

As Nicodemus said, *"We can no longer live as rats. We know too much."* We must ascend into the role of the pied piper and free ourselves of the rats among us who've been the plague on our "movements" and who've corrupted authentic discourse to the brink of no return. Like the pied piper, that there is an ambiguity in our own righteousness and in ascertaining whom we can trust— if even ourselves—is something we must be willing to accept, and just serenade on. Continue to push forward anyway, *no matter what*. If by "coincidence" we hit on a string of bad luck, we just have to laugh it off and shrug our shoulders. *Me ne frego!*

People can *try* to forget what they've learned and attempt to fade back into the ordinary world, keeping their heads down and live-action roleplaying as average Joes living virtuous normie lives. I can't say I really blame them. Dissident politics is filled with abrasive and deranged people. Being constantly prodded and probed like a lab rat by the government and eyeballed by every open eye like an animal in the zoo only adds to the distress. Maybe some of those who take a stab at pacified living will even be able to maintain the charade, having convinced themselves they're making a difference by "being the change they want to see in the world," by going to church every Sunday and becoming active at local PTA meetings (for as long as they are still held in intelligible English.) Wholesome trad communities and white women in wheat fields are all fun and games until the government dumps a few thousand Somali refugees into the neighborhood.

The rest of us may be guilty of abandoning our passions periodically, when the strain of solving torturous math problems by other means unleashes a psychic descent into madness too difficult to bear. Yet, with those nagging thoughts still gnawing away at us like electric blue wiring of the clearest variety, in deep midnight moments of chlorinated clarity, and our repressed passions relenting to the tidal force of an illuminated moon, we will time and time again find ourselves drawn back toward facing what we sense in our hearts to be true.

About the Author

Brandon Adamson is a writer from Phoenix, Arizona

Works Cited

Alonzo, Monica. "Inside the Phoenix PD's Use of Federal Anti-
Terrorism Resources to Track Valley Protesters." *Phoenix New
Times*, 20 June 2013.
https://www.phoenixnewtimes.com/news/inside-the-
phoenix-pds-use-of-federal-anti-terrorism-resources-to-
track-valley-protesters-6458962

Bond, Paul. "NBC News Fires Third Employee Over Doctored   911
Call in Trayvon Martin Controversy." *The Hollywood
Reporter*, 3 May 2012,
www.hollywoodreporter.com/news/trayvon-martin-nbc-
news-fires-third-employee-319991.

Elstad, Peter L. "Overcoming Information Operations Legal Limitations
in Support of Domestic Operations." Hsdl.org Homeland
Security Digital Library at NPS, U.S. Army Command and
General Staff College, 12 Dec. 2008, www.hsdl.org/?
abstract&did=17753

"Affidavit In Support of An Application For a Search Warrant"
United States v. 8ch.net. No. 19MJ1755. District Court,
S.D. California. 29 Apr. 2019.
https://www.courtlistener.com/recap/gov.uscourts.casd.626722
/gov.uscourts.casd.626722.1.0.pdf

"Inspired by Tarrant shooting muslims." /pol/ Politically Incorrect
(Archived Thread) 8chan , 29 Apr. 2019, archive.is/YJzmC.

Wingerter, Meg. "Regret and unanswered questions swirl as Varnell
bombing case progresses." *The Oklahoman*, 11 Jan. 2018,
www.oklahoman.com/article/5576064/regret-and-
unanswered-questions-swirl-as-varnell-bombing-case- progresses.

Winston, Ali. "For Charlottesville Authorities, a Painful Post- Mortem on
Preparedness." *PBS/ProPublica* , 11 Jan. 2018,
www.pbs.org/wgbh/frontline/article/for-charlottesville-
authorities-a-painful-post-mortem-on-preparedness/. Accessed 7
Aug. 2018.

"'Winning' and Candy Land." YouTube, Pilleater (Francis Nally), 10 Jan.
2019, www.youtube.com/watch?v=GAJEpL7jdQk

"Criminalizing Mental Illness." YouTube, Ramzpaul (Paul Ramsey), 7
Aug. 2019, www.youtube.com/watch?v=YtOtb7_WcNI.

Davis, Kelly. "Shell Shock." *San Diego CityBeat*, 2 Mar. 2010,
sdcitybeat.com/news-and-opinion/news/shell-shock/.

Counterfeit World: Making 'To Live and Die in L.A.' (Video 2003).
(2003, December 2). Retrieved from
https://www.imdb.com/title/tt0404891

Stonor Saunders, Francis. "Modern Art Was CIA 'weapon'." *The Independent*, 22, Oct. 1995, www.independent.co.uk/news/world/modern-art-was-cia-weapon-1578808.html.

"Nixon: "The Jews Are Born Spies"." *Miller Center*, 24 Feb. 2017, millercenter.org/the-presidency/educational- resources/nixon-the-jews-are-born-spies.

Laliberte, B. (2019, April 30). How The Illuminati Fucked Up My Life. Retrieved from web.archive.org/web/20190430131223/ https://theamericansun.co m/2019/04/30/how-the-illuminati-fucked-up-my-life

Liddell, C. (2019, June 19). FEDERAL BUDGET TO INCREASE AFTER COMEDIAN WINS $4.1 MILLION LAWSUIT AGAINST ANGLIN. http://trad-news.blogspot.com/2019/06/federal-budget-to-increase-after.html

"Kinds of Torture Endured in Ritual Abuse and Trauma-Based Mind Control." *End Ritual Abuse*, 29 June 2017, endritualabuse.org/kinds-of-torture-endured-in-ritual-abuse-and-trauma-based-mind-control/

"Origins and Techniques of Monarch Mind Control." *The Vigilant Citizen*, 2 Oct. 2018, vigilantcitizen.com/hidden-knowledge/origins-and-techniques-of-monarch-mind-control/

BEYOND THE ICE CREAM SEA

The micromoon's tidal forces,
an inflatable holographic chair,
the boardgame *Candy Land* (1984 version)
no strategy involved just chance of the cards

photograph from a
vintage camera with a
scratch on the lens
    interesting

also
a blue otter pop
fresh from the freezer

and random
dancefloor of emotion that lights up and
dynamically changes with the clearest music

matching "glow in the dark" decoder rings
a temporary tattoo parlor
translucent image
of what? a rat?
fades fast in a cold shower

a certain kind of wearer

makes a one day waterpark wristband

   last

       all

           summer

  anyway

nothing it's just a cool color

ha

nervous laughter

Made in the USA
Columbia, SC
30 December 2019